THE MANY PARTS OF YOU

Understanding the puzzle of your behaviour

Foreword written by Gordon Emmerson PhD

JAN SKY

BALBOA
PRESS

A DIVISION OF HAY HOUSE

Balboa Press books may be ordered through booksellers or by contacting:

Balboa Press
A Division of Hay House
1663 Liberty Drive
Bloomington, IN 47403
www.balboapress.com.au
1-(877) 407-4847

ISBN: 978-1-4525-0766-8 (sc)
ISBN: 978-1-4525-0767-5 (e)

Because of the dynamic nature of the Internet, any web addresses or
links contained in this book may have changed since publication and may
no longer be valid. The views expressed in this work are solely those
of the author and do not necessarily reflect the views of the publisher,
and the publisher hereby disclaims any responsibility for them.

The author of this book does not dispense medical advice or prescribe the
use of any technique as a form of treatment for physical, emotional, or medical
problems without the advice of a physician, either directly or indirectly. The
intent of the author is only to offer information of a general nature to help you
in your quest for emotional and spiritual well-being. In the event you use any
of the information in this book for yourself, which is your constitutional right,
the author and the publisher assume no responsibility for your actions.

Any people depicted in stock imagery provided by Thinkstock are models,
and such images are being used for illustrative purposes only.
Certain stock imagery © Thinkstock.

Printed in the United States of America

Balboa Press rev. date: 10/23/2012

Dedication

Dedicated to my friend of 51 years, Sandra,
who disclosed, without realising, the many
parts of her.

Thank you.

Executive State
Identification ESI is a psycho-analytical tool developed and trialled by Jan Sky since 2006 with outstanding results. These trials, primarily in prisons, continue as does her work today. ESI enables you to identify a map of who you are—your states—and to identify inhibiting states which are to be moved aside and replaced with states that promote success in the individual.

Contents

Foreword

"Part of me would like to, but another part knows I had better not." How often have you said or heard something like that?

We all know, intuitively, that our psyches are made up of different parts. Our parts are even common in our language, as we talk about our parts and the inner voices. One part of us can even like or love a person, while another part does not. It is not unusual for a person to reflect in their mind upon previous discussions between parts, when considering whether to stay with a partner, or leave. Even buying a pair of shoes or a new car can create a discussion between two of our parts. One part may say, "I like it, and I want it" while another part may say, "It's too expensive. I can't afford it."

Paul Federn was a contemporary of Freud but, unlike Freud who saw the personality as having only three parts—the Id, the Ego, and the Superego—Federn saw the personality as having a number of parts. He called the parts 'ego states', because as we switch from one state to another our ego identity goes with us. That is why when we are in the part that likes the new car we say to ourselves, "I like it," and while we are in the part that looks after the bank account we say to ourselves, "I can't afford it." While in each part—the hedonistic part that wants the car, or the accountant part that looks after the bank balance—we feel, "this is me." Our ego identity goes with us into whichever part is executive, or whichever state we are in.

Ego State Therapy is a relatively new and growing therapeutic orientation. World Congresses have been held about this subject in Germany (2003) and in South Africa (2006). It is interesting to note how the movement made its way into this new and creative book. During the first half of the 20th century psychoanalysis was the favoured psychotherapeutic orientation. It has long been the practice that to be a psychoanalyst the therapist needs to first go through psychoanalysis. An Italian man, Edoardo Weiss, in order to become a psychoanalyst himself, chose Paul Federn as his psychoanalyst. Weiss was fascinated with Federn's ideas. He learned from Federn his ideas about ego states, and about how the personality is divided into distinct states that, when either comes into executive, enable an ego identity to be invested. His belief in these ideas resulted in his editing and publishing Federn's writings (after Federn's death) in the book, *Ego Psychology and the Psychoses* (Federn, 1952).

Also in the 1950s, John Watkins entered psychoanalysis so he could become a psychoanalyst. Watkins had already published a book on War Neuroses (1949) and, after choosing Weiss as his analyst and learning about ego states from him, Watkins' own body of work took on a new and clearer meaning. He realised that he had been working with ego states for a number of years, while helping soldiers who had returned from World War II. He had helped them resolve their traumatised ego states, thereby eliminating their hysteric symptoms. This was some of the first work conducted with ego states relating to trauma.

John Watkins, together with his wife Helen, can be thought of as the father and mother of Ego State Therapy. Their book, *Ego States: Theory and Therapy,* (1997) and their many articles written during and following the 1970s, built Federn's and Weiss's notions of ego states into a theory of personality, and a viable therapeutic orientation.

Among the many contributors to the development and understanding of this new field were Frederick, Phillips, Hartman, McNeal, Morton, Kluft, Torem, Fraser, Hunter,

Gainer, and Forgash. My own contributions have consisted of articles, workshops, and two books. Having spent the summer of 2000 with the Watkinses in Missoula, and having conducted a diploma-level course that Jan Sky completed, the lineage from the first understandings of ego states to this book is clear: Federn, Weiss, Watkins, Emmerson, Sky.

This book is at the cutting edge of the evolving applications of ego state theory. Sky has developed a process she calls Executive State Identification (ESI). This process is used to bring about behavioural changes by locating and working with individual ego states. A first step in this process is for readers to learn to map their ego states. To this end, Sky presents a number of techniques that assist readers to better understand the specific parts they have. Each person has an idiosyncratic ego state map, and no two people have the same states that communicate together in the same way. Therefore, Sky's mapping process is an important step toward self-awareness and empowerment.

Sky sees the process of ESI as being beneficial in the workplace, increasing staff morale, decreasing internal conflict, increasing revenue, decreasing staff turnover, increasing productivity, and decreasing absenteeism. It follows that, if staff are able to understand themselves better, heal their fragile, reactive parts, and gain better access to their best parts for each activity, a more productive milieu would result. Sky provides examples and case studies to better illustrate this.

Conscientious readers of this book will gain much in self-understanding and in an ability to feel more control in their lives. Just as Ego State Therapy provides rapid movement for the client by focusing directly on the states in which the cause of an issue resides, ESI provides a way for individuals to better understand themselves and better use the specific inner resources available to them.

For example, it would be a real waste to go on a bush walk in a business ego state and use that time to worry about the work that needed to be done in the office. Rather, it would be best be in an ego state that could appreciate nature and use the time to build positive energy and gratitude for beauty. Likewise, work productivity would suffer if, while at work, staff were unfocused and wishing to be elsewhere, rather than in a productive state that could focus on the task at hand and appreciate a movement in accomplishing that task.

This book provides an additional step in applying ego state theory. It is my belief that ego state theory will find its way into a vast array of personal, social and cultural applications. The reader of this book will discover that the utility of understanding our states is vast.

Gordon Emmerson, PhD

Dr Emmerson is a senior lecturer in psychology at Victoria University in Melbourne

Preface

Jan Sky has taken Ego State Therapy techniques into the workplace. She has provided a simple and effective way of using Ego State Identification as a means of identifying the parts that make up an individual's identity.

Jan not only identifies the ego states, she demonstrates how to use that knowledge to help one to create change.

The implications for one's professional and personal life are huge. Reactionary? Proactionary? Knowing what ego states one has means freedom of choice of behaviour and emotions.

Jan Sky has presented case histories that are simple to understand and that provide evidence of the effectiveness of Ego State Identification.

Once states are mapped, options are apparent, giving the ability to choose which state is to be in the executive; thereby affecting behaviour and emotions, and creating change and different responses at will.

The significant work of John and Helen Watkins in the area of Ego State Therapy has been with us for some years and is more readily available since the publication of their book, *Ego States: Theory and Therapy (1997)*.

Gordon Emmerson, through his books, *Ego State Therapy (2003)* and *Advanced Skills and Interventions in Therapeutic Counseling (2006)*, and his in-depth teaching of Ego State Therapy in Australia and internationally, has brought the knowledge of this therapeutic technique to many.

Roy Hunter, who wrote *Hypnosis for Inner Conflict Resolution: Introducing Parts Therapy (1995)* has added more information and weight to the subject.

'Parts' or 'ego states' have often been confused with the Parent, Adult, Child ego states of Transactional Analysis (TA). There is a vast difference, and yet those TA ego states can be evident in the ego states identified when ego state mapping is done.

The information contained in this book will benefit many. Employers, employees and anyone working in groups (or even individually) will gain the knowledge that a person's behaviour is not 100% of the person; just one aspect or part that is in the executive, or operating system, at any one time, and that another, more co-operative, part has the potential to be accessed and moved into the executive role.

It puts one in charge of one's life. How good is that!

Lyn MacIntosh

Counsellor, Hypnotherapist, NLP Master Practitioner

Introduction

Solve the puzzle of your behaviour by understanding the many parts of you that make up who you are. Once this is achieved, you are able to nominate those parts that inhibit your progress and those that support success in your life. It is then easier to acknowledge what behaviour changes are needed to be made and, with practice, make those changes stick!

This book is based on the process called ESI—Executive State Identification.

For more than 25 years, I have been involved in training, mostly in the interactive area of communications, either by team building, conflict resolution or customer service, working with organisations and their people to move change. Addressing behavioural changes has been my primary objective because I believe that you couldn't simply run a training course and expect change, you needed to work with people after the training to ensure change.

Developing ESI enabled me to identify the behaviour of an individual and, by breaking the behaviour into 'parts', I was better able to identify which 'part' they were operating from and therefore which part of the individual needed changing. These 'parts' I called STATES. I was working from the premise that not 'all of the person' needed changing, just the inhibiting part or state. The state from which the person's behaviour is demonstrated is called the Executive State. If the executive state was inappropriate to the enhancement of good relationships, that state needed to be identified and its existence justified. A state identification allowed the individual to gain self-awareness and this would lead to the 'reshuffling' of states to bring about behavioural change—change that was necessary to positively affect the fundamental workings of the individual.

An ESI process is conducted with the individual's input and involvement, and this in itself makes the process a very powerful one, as it allows the individual to take ownership and work towards achieving their goals.

Small businesses through to large corporations suffer the downfall of individuals who are not committed to 'the workplace goals', who are acting out through inappropriate executive states, thus ultimately making the journey to the goal harder and longer.

So, what is ESI?

ESI (Executive State Identification) is a tool which can easily be used in a conscious way to bring about behavioural changes and to allow those changes to stick! These changes in behaviour will ultimately enhance an individual's level of success, happiness, awareness and achievement, particularly when focussed on achieving goals.

ESI has been developed from the work of 'ego states' by such theorists as Dr Gordon Emmerson, Paul Federn, John and Helen Watkins, and others. ESI clearly delineates 'states' or parts of us that represent our conscious moods and form part of our cognitive thinking. Such states could be identified as anger, fear, elation, frustration and jubilation, to name a few, and each of the states have roles. For example, if we are acting out of the state of ANGER, the role of ANGER could be to make us yell out, hit the other person, call the other person by an offensive name. When we are 'acting out' of such a state, the state is identified as an 'executive state'. Executive states contribute to our behaviour in any given situation, as identified when describing how the roles of anger are defined.

For example, a therapist would use Ego State Therapy with a client in an induced state of trance (hypnosis) to explore and **map** that client's states. The use of hypnosis allows you to identify executive, non executive and underlying states. Once a 'State Map' has been created of your own unique profile you are in a position of awareness and a rearrangement of states to achieve goals can then take place. All of this is facilitated and encouraged by the therapist.

> **From Gordon Emmerson PhD, Ego State Therapy, Crown House Publishing (2003):**

> *Ego state therapy is based on the premise that personality is composed of separate parts, rather than being a homogenous whole. These parts (which everyone has) are called ego states. The state that is conscious and overt at any time is referred to as the executive state. Some non-executive ego states will be consciously aware of what is happening, while others may be unconscious and unaware.* Chapter 1, page 1.

Our unconscious contains our ego states that are underlying and non executive—some of which may not have been executive for many years. They maintain their own memory and communicate with other ego states to a greater or lesser degree.

States are identified as **executive**, **non executive** and **underlying**.

Executive states contribute to our behaviour, thereby allowing us to function externally with other individuals. For example, a customer service person conducting a transaction, or a staff member deciding whether or not to apply for a promotion, are both people who would be acting from a particular state or behaving in a particular way, i.e. operating in an executive state. Only one state is the executive state at any given time, however, states may switch to the executive rapidly and/or support each other when needed. Refer to Chapter Two for customer service experience.

Non executive states are those that contribute to our behaviour on a regular basis as we move in and out of various daily situations. When not in executive they support other states, particularly those in executive at any given moment.

Underlying states are those that rarely come to the executive. They vary greatly in their relative closeness to the behaviour of the individual, yet can be identified as supporting the other states (executive and non executive). Underlying states were discovered by Dr Gordon Emmerson, as referred to in his book Ego State Therapy (2003). They are more easily identified through the process of hypnosis. Using ESI, both executive and non executive states can be identified. I have experienced occasions, using ESI, when my clients have identified underlying states and the results have been outstanding. Underlying states are often formed in early childhood as a protection mechanism and can become executive at inappropriate times in adult situations. However, underlying states mostly remain hidden in our subconscious.

Mapping of states refers to the identification of states within. This concept was also developed by Dr Emmerson and it includes learning about the internal relationship of the states and roles, or the profiles of the states. Mapping enables a person to have a better self-understanding, to become more self-aware. Conducted at a conscious level, mapping will easily identify those states that operate in executive.

A role of the states refers to what that state allows you to do. For example, as stated above, the role of ANGER was to hit the other person, yell out, and call the other person by offensive names. There is a state of ANGER in most individuals; however the distinguishing difference is in the role of the state. Your state of ANGER could have quite different roles to the one referred to in this instance.

The ESI process does not require one to be put into a state of trance and involves a series of questions, referred to by Dr Gordon Emmerson (2003) as 'conversational technique', to establish what conscious states a person is operating in at any given time. It is designed to establish if these states are supportive of a person's current position in life.

Self-Talk Dialogue: This is a personal phrase or affirmation developed at the end of an ESI process from the realisation of one's own State Map. It serves as a reminder of which states to operate from, when they feel those inhibiting states rising inside them. This 'self-talk' dialogue is powerful to the individual because it is personal and relates directly to them. It's their own personal, positive affirmation. The process of ESI is simple and effective, enabling changes to occur naturally and uniquely.

Goals of ESI

The goals of an ESI process are:

o To locate the states that harbour anger, pain or frustration or limiting beliefs, and facilitate acknowledgment, which enhances satisfaction and empowerment
o To facilitate functional communication between states
o To enable people to identify their own states and the roles of those states, and
o To develop a 'self-talk' dialogue to enhance desired change.

Benefits of ESI

Developing an understanding of 'the many parts of you', your states and their roles will:

o   Increase a person's awareness of their personality, and
o   Provide an avenue to affect rapid and lasting change.

ESI is a proven, powerful tool that will allow effective changes to occur in individuals, teams and organisations. You can experience an ESI process yourself or learn how to use this unique tool by becoming an ESI practitioner. As a practitioner, you would expect to improve upon your coaching, performance management, counselling, training, HR, and/or team leading skills and add to your personal skill profile.

This book will take you on a journey of discovery and reveal maps of others who, using ESI, have made significant changes to their behaviours and, consequently, their lives. It will also give you the opportunity to explore your own map and apply behavioural changes to yourself.

Enjoy the book and the learning experiences that are shared.

Chapter One—Motivation and Mary

Observing ESI in action

I was given the opportunity to support a woman who was searching for the daughter she had given up for adoption 22 years ago. My task was to facilitate this reunion. There was a certain amount of urgency around this reunion as the mother, Mary, had been diagnosed with a terminal illness. My role was to meet with Mary to determine her needs, provide counselling where necessary and play a part in the meeting. This included communicating with the daughter and unfolding her needs as well.

On my first visit with Mary, I found a pale-skinned woman being fed through a tube inserted into her nose, who needed an oxygen mask to breathe and had not been out of bed, except when assisted for the essentials, in three months. Mary was unable to walk, had a chronic heart condition, failing internal functioning and was operating on just one kidney—and it wasn't doing too well either! Just to name a few disorders!

We discussed her needs concerning the proposed reunion and I determined that, although she wanted to meet her daughter, she was concerned about her illnesses and how she looked. What would her daughter think, say, and/or do? How could she accept her in this way?

"I never wanted to give her away in the first place. Friends convinced me that I couldn't possibly look after her", she told me, and the tears flowed.

Between my first and second visit the daughter's personal information was sourced from the archives of the Department of Children's Services. Mary's daughter had begun her own search for her mum about eight years prior, however, at that point Mary hadn't responded to any form of contact. As for her daughter, she had known all of her life that she was adopted and was fortunately supported by her adoptive parents in her search for her birth mother when and if she was ready. Photos and letters had been sent to Mary during her daughter's growing years and now, at 22 years of age and with a five-year-old daughter of her own, the pieces of the jigsaw were being placed into position.

It was on my second visit with Mary that the miracles started to unfold.

Miracle No 1: The day after my first visit, Mary had requested the nursing staff help her out of her bed and into a wheelchair.

Miracle No 2: She had insisted the tube be removed from her nose and told the nursing staff she wanted to eat by herself.

Miracle No 3: She was wearing a sweater and track pants, instead of a nightie.

Miracles indeed, especially considering the seriousness of her condition!

What was it that had enabled Mary to achieve all this? Well, obviously the prospect of meeting her daughter! The executive state Mary was operating from was her MOTIVATING state. Although there had been many other opportunities over the years, the timing then hadn't been right—now it was. She wanted to meet her daughter and didn't want to be in a bed, in pyjamas and looking the way she did, she explained to me.

Contact through DOCS had been made with the daughter, who was overjoyed with excitement, and the meeting date was set. Mary had requested my presence at the meeting, along with her social worker—a wonderful woman who had supported her through many years of difficulties. Mary wanted doughnuts and coffee served and also wanted to be taken to the shops in the hospital prior to the meeting. Coffee and doughnuts was a bit of a problem (we **were** in a hospital) however, her social worker did accompany her to the shops where she purchased nail polish and makeup.

The day of the meeting

A phone call to Mary on the way to the hospital revealed a very excited woman and, on arrival I was witness to yet another miracle. Mary was in her wheelchair, dressed in a long black skirt with a purple top; her hair tied back with a mauve ribbon; nails painted, lipstick to match and looking just gorgeous. Nothing like the woman I had seen just one week prior.

She chose to hold her oxygen mask rather than have the elastic around her head—not to mess her hair, she explained, and I noticed that she was using the oxygen less and less.

Her daughter's entrance triggered a flow of tears. Mary was overcome with a mass of mixed feelings and emotions. Such an emotional experience! In that very moment you could actually feel an outpouring of love. It was sensational! With semi-dry eyes, the two began to talk and ask questions of each other, exchanging gestures and events of their lives. Their similarities were remarkable and, for the next two hours, I witnessed such a wonderful example of how the many parts of Mary had worked in her favour for this meeting with her daughter to occur.

Just one hour into the reunion I noticed **Miracle No 5:** Mary had dropped her oxygen mask to the floor and was breathing unaided. When I questioned her she replied that it was better off 'down there' than on her face.

3

Jan Sky

As I left them on that day, Mary, her daughter and her daughter's partner were heading for the hospital coffee shop—daughter pushing Mary in the wheelchair and partner wheeling the unattached oxygen tank—a security measure that the nursing staff insisted upon!

The courage to do this was found by letting her desire grow larger than her fear. She found the strength in her unique map of states that gave her a 'longing to live' and 'a willingness to settle for nothing less'.

Mary had, for many years, been operating from executive states that didn't support her desire to meet with her daughter. This time, when the opportunity to meet her daughter presented itself again, Mary did her own executive state reshuffle. Rather than functioning from an unmotivated place where she was drowning in her own illnesses, using states that had the roles of feeling 'I'm not good enough', 'fear', and 'regret'—just to name a few—her executive state reshuffle brought to the surface such states that had the roles of 'I'm okay', 'love' and 'motivation'. These states had been underlying for such a long time, allowing the more negative states to act out in an executive role and control her behaviour.

MOTIVATION appeared to be the executive state that drove Mary to achieve her fullest potential. When she reshuffled her states from living in the executive states of FEAR or DESPAIR and replaced them with the executive state of MOTIVATION, her behaviour changed—as well as her attitude!

We are all aware that to do anything in life we need to have motivation. The more motivated we are the more effective we tend to be. When our motivation is aligned with our 'higher-self' our capacity to achieve is increased and the end results are often greater than anticipated.

On this occasion, I was witness to behavioural changes that had been inspired by an executive state that carried the roles appropriate to Mary's success. In just one week, Mary was able to achieve remarkable results in spite of her disabilities.

Do you let your disabilities get in your way? Do you continue to operate on a daily basis from executive states that are unproductive and inappropriate for your higher sense of self?

- *Be motivated to achieve and create your own miracles.*

- *Be prepared to identify what executive states govern your thinking and control your behaviour.*

- *Be prepared to identify what executive states inhibit your achievement.*

- *Be prepared to partake in an executive state reshuffle.*

EXERCISE:

GOAL: _____

Make your goal a **SMART** goal:

Specific—be clear about what you want

Measurable—a goal that can be measured in terms of how long it will take to achieve it

Action plan—create and action plan around the goal

Real for you, **realistic**—be sure this goal is really one that you want to achieve

Timely, **time-line**—is it the right time in your life and can you create a time-line towards it?

"What is the part of me that wants to achieve this goal?"

NAME OF PART: _____

"Is there a part of me that is holding me back from achieving this goal?"

NAME OF PART: _____

Chapter Two—Identification of States

"Part of me wants to go to the party tonight and part of me wants to stay at home!"

Sound familiar?

Here is a very simple example of identifying the many parts of you . . .

In deciding what to do, you identify the part of you that really wants to go to the party. For example, this particular part may love the company of others, enjoy having fun and be looking forward to seeing particular people there. To identify that state, you need to focus on that part of you that 'really wants to go to the party' and give it a name. Giving it a name simply allows you to identify that part now and in the future. For example, the name could be FUN.

The next step is to ask yourself, "what role does FUN play out for me?"

FUN may have the roles of:

- o   allowing you to laugh
- o   allowing you to be silly
- o   enjoying the company of others
- o   feeling good

These are really important roles and you probably feel fantastic when FUN is in executive state.

Now identify the part of you that doesn't want to go to the party. For example, this part may dislike one or two of the guests who will be attending, may not want to drink alcohol tonight, may feel a little off-colour. Focus on that part of you that doesn't want to go to the party and give it a name. You might name this one SENSIBLE.

Again, ask yourself, "What role does SENSIBLE play out for me?"

SENSIBLE may have the roles of:

- o   preventing you from drinking too much alcohol
- o   not allowing you to make a fool of yourself
- o   helping you make the *right* decisions

These are very important roles too, and need to be acknowledged. You would probably feel like you are in control when SENSIBLE is in executive.

In this identification process, there could be a link between the two states. Some questions to ask would be; "Could SENSIBLE support FUN if you chose to go to the party? If so, how?"

States that are identified as 'executive'

It is said that we operate between five to 15 executive states throughout a normal week/month. These states represent the personality of the individual and usually communicate well with each other. When we switch from one state to another we generally remember what happened and what we were doing in the previous state, although this memory is not always complete.

An excerpt from Gordon Emmerson's book, *Ego State Therapy (2003)*, describes this perfectly (page 5):

> *". . . When we walk from watching television into the kitchen and open the refrigerator door we often switch from a relaxing/spectator state to a more functional/ doer state. We are able to remember where we came from (the other room) and what we were doing (watching TV), but occasionally we may not remember why we came into the kitchen. When we sit for an exam in a nervous state we may not remember well the things we learned in a relaxed state, but if we are able to switch into the state we studied in, our recall will be much better."*

Executive states are said to be our conscious behaviour which allows us to function externally with other individuals. "A state is one of a group of similar states, each distinguished by a particular role, mood and mental function, which when conscious assumes first person identity." (Emmerson, 2003)

Let me use an example such as a customer service transaction. If the person providing the customer service wanted to please the customer and carry out the transaction in the best possible way, an executive state from which they might operate could be one that has the role of being confident or wanting to please. The customer might be operating from the executive state that has the role of gratitude.

On the contrary, if the salesperson was becoming annoyed with the customer, the executive state might have the role of being rude or not caring about successfully completing the transaction.

The customer, too, would be influenced by this behaviour and move from a state that had the role of gratitude to an executive state reflecting that of the salesperson, which engaged the role of annoyance, for example.

Executive states form our thinking and consequent behaviour, and in an instant a situation can be transformed from positive to negative or vice versa. Having an awareness of your State Map and choosing to operate from those states that benefit and enhance positive situations ultimately achieves success.

It is said that only one state is in the executive state at any given time. However, my belief—based on experiences I've gathered from clients—is that states may switch to the executive from non executive rapidly, and/or support each other when needed.

Apart from the small range of states from which we usually operate, there are many more states that we have used in past situations. When our salesperson (described above) was dealing with the customer in an appropriate manner, operating from a state that carried the role of confidence and wanting to satisfy, the customer may have inadvertently said something that triggered a memory from their past. An underlying state that experienced a conflict situation could be pushed into an executive role simply by hearing the words the customer spoke. This would then change both the behaviour of the salesperson and, in turn, the entire dynamics of the transaction.

Having an understanding of our states (and their sources, where possible) enables us to have greater control over our behaviour because we are able to draw from our State Map those states appropriate to enhance situations, rather than impede them.

It is essential to say at this point that when we operate from any given executive state it becomes obvious through our behaviour and consequently our tone of voice and body language. Observe a person operating out of an executive state who is reliving a particular childhood experience or event. Apart from hearing the story you can observe changes in their tone of voice and body language. They may be excited, use a higher pitched voice, giggle, make their body appear smaller and act in an unadult-like manner. These key communication signals assist in identifying state changes.

States that are identified as 'non executive'

A non executive state is one of a group of states that are not in executive at the given moment. They are part of the five to 15 states that we operate between in any given week/month. Non executive states can go into executive in an instant and they are often known to support other states, particularly those in executive.

Underlying states are states that come to the executive rarely. They vary greatly in their relative closeness to the behaviour of the individual and rarely communicate with executive states. These states become executive only occasionally and are difficult to identify unless they become executive. It is understood that most underlying states hold positive and pleasant memories as well as unresolved trauma. An underlying state could come into executive when an old memory was revisited such as a smell of a chocolate box or the sounds of childish giggles. Some of these memories may have previously been unknown to the executive states.

It is sometimes only possible to access underlying states through the assistance of a therapist while using hypnotherapy as the tool. However, it has been my experience, using ESI, that underlying states have come to the surface and clients have experienced huge breakthroughs.

Each one of the hundreds of clients I have had the privilege to work with experienced huge self-awareness, which has given them opportunities to look more closely at themselves. In doing so, they identify parts of them that they really weren't aware existed until that ESI process was conducted with them.

I would suggest that we breeze through life doing much the same thing day after day—whether in the workplace, with our families or socially—and spend very little time taking a closer look at our many parts. We identify that we are made up of different parts and yet through habit, or simply comfort, operate the same, day after day. This can be a good thing and most people don't question their own actions. However, consider wanting more from life, or seeing a new possibility—would your existing states support the changes that you would need to make in order to achieve what you wanted?

Unless you are very well-equipped at knowing the many parts that make up who you are, I would suggest not.

We can write business plans, create fantastic marketing objectives, engage the help of others and, given the right conditions, success can be ours. Let's say that you do all or some of these and yet still don't make your goal. Can you then identify the 'part of you' that is holding you back?

An ESI process can do exactly this and will ensure the necessary behaviour changes occur to achieve your goals.

Here is an example of ESI at work with a CEO of an organisation.

COACHING CLIENT

A client I was coaching recently, who had completed an Apollo Profile had displayed low in decision-making skills. He seemed to be too cautious and therefore most likely too slow in decision-making, probably wanting every last bit of data before deciding.

As my client was the CEO of an organisation, his perceived hesitation to make a decision generated feelings of frustration and, at times, annoyance in other senior executives and senior management staff. We discussed the need for him to keep his people informed, i.e. communicate regularly with them and/or explain the reason for the delayed decision and give them a date (where possible) that the decision will be made by.

In further discussion I asked my client if he was a risk-taker, to which he replied 'yes, however mostly out of the workplace'. My client climbed cliff faces, wind surfed in the surf and was an avid skier. Slipping easily into ESI mode, I asked him the roles of 'risk-taker' and he explained that when he was taking risks he felt challenged (in a positive way); a sense of anxiety and excitement at the same time and was much more focussed.

I proceeded to ask what it would take to bring those same skills to the workplace, (i.e. challenge, anxiety, excitement, focus) and he came up with the quote, "Focus on benefits of having made the decision".

"How powerful this was", I thought! The next thing my client did was to make this a 'pop up' in his Outlook, so he was regularly reminded of how he could take risks at work and make decisions a little more quickly.

Chapter Three—Mapping of States

Mapping of states refers to the identification of states within. This includes learning the internal relationship of the states and their roles or profiles. Mapping enables a person to have a better self-understanding or self-awareness. Although we all have the three state types—executive, non executive and underlying, no two people have the same states with roles that are the same. A State Map is a map of our individual identity and gives us a better insight into our behaviour patterns.

When creating a State Map, we are identifying those states that are executive and non executive and contribute to our behaviour on a daily basis, or in particular situations. They explain our normal functioning. Mostly, these states have good communication between each other, however there are times when states are in conflict, and I hasten to point out that this is when a State Map has a real purpose. To simply create a map of well-communicating states holds little purpose except for identification; it is when we find ourselves in a state of frustration, unable to make a decision or in pain or conflict that a State Map has meaning.

It is important to differentiate between 'states' and 'multiple personalities'. It isn't uncommon for people to think of multiple personalities when they are first introduced to Executive State Identification. There are major differences between Dissociative Identity Disorder or Multiple Personality and ESI. While we all have states, Multiple Personalities are quite different and develop in only a small minority of cases, for example, when a young child experiences extreme abuse continuing over an extended period of time.

When some children experience chronic abuse, as an unconscious coping mechanism, there is a breakdown of communication between the ego states so that the child can experience the next day without memory of the abuse the night before. Some children, therefore, learn to 'not remember' what happened while in their previous ego state. Over time, they can become so proficient at this 'not remembering' that the ego states become separated in communication. Hence the term 'multiple personality'. When this happens, each state has to learn to take on a fuller range of roles as it cannot easily call on other states or retain a memory of what happened while in a previous state. People who have multiple personalities experience periods of 'blackout' during their day, because often when they switch personalities they have no memory of what they were doing, or why they were doing it, just moments before.

While a person with normal state identification may walk from the lounge room to the bathroom, open the cabinet door and think, "why did I come in here?", a person with multiple personalities may open the cabinet door and think, "why am I here, how long have I been here, where was I before, and what was I doing?"

Creating an Executive State Map

When creating a State Map, it is important that you deal with only one state at a time and 'tease out' the roles of that particular state. States have a purpose (role) and every state requires appropriate acknowledgment for its purpose.

With my work with inmates in prison, I am often dealing with the executive state of ANGER or a state that has the role of anger. Anger is a complex emotion that all human beings experience and often find confusing. Anger causes confusion because it is often viewed as behaviour. It is equated with violence, withholding, demanding, aggression, meanness, hurt and/ or cruelty, rather than as a feeling. People have behavioural responses to anger, but anger is not behaviour; anger is an emotional state.

Using the process of ESI, the men I worked with were encouraged to identify executive states and discover the advantages and disadvantages of each of them. Together we have worked through the process of what the roles of these states are; when and why these states are in executive, and the appropriate use of executive states. Mostly, my findings have been that there was disharmony between the states and the process of ESI has helped harmonise their lives by creating an executive state profile. Positive, functional emotional states, once identified, support appropriate behavioural changes when brought into executive.

David was a prison inmate who was a very angry young man; it was probably his anger that put him into prison in the first instance and he was still displaying signs of anger when I met him. I asked David to think of an incident where he had felt extreme anger—now that wasn't a difficult task! I didn't need to know the incident if he chose not to tell me, all I wanted him to do was identify the many parts of himself and also to identify their roles. We worked with this and I then asked him to identify other emotional states that were present at the same time as ANGER. These states were identified and their roles were acknowledged. See diagram below.

ANGER
Role:

- o   To be confronting
- o   To criticise

RAGE
Role:

- o   To allow me to be heard
- o   To let off steam
- o   To be better than the other person

COURAGE
Role:

- o   To help me feel strong
- o   To give me confidence

FEAR
Role:

- o   To help rage make a noise
- o   To support rage

STUPID
Role:

- o   To feel embarrassment
- o   To look like a fool

CONTROL
Role:

   o   To support courage
   o   To be in charge

The next step was to create a State Map around the incident and draw a link between those states that worked together. David and I worked through this process. See chart (i) for the State Map:

Chart (i) State Map

A body of behaviours and experiences bound together by a common incident, lines drawn between states indicate those that are linked and/or support each other.

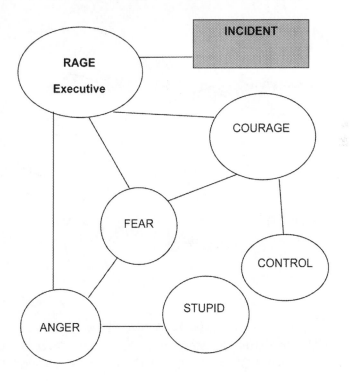

This ESI mapping process revealed five states that supported RAGE when RAGE was in executive, and from this David clearly identified how inappropriate some of these states were if, in the future, he wanted a more positive outcome. We explored the possibility of disconnecting the states of COURAGE and CONTROL from RAGE and putting them into executive when a similar incident occurred in the future. David agreed with that concept. He also identified another state, that of DECISION MAKER, and its role was to give him a choice with a response. Should a similar incident occur I would suggest his State Map (chart ii) would look something like this:

Chart (ii) New State Map

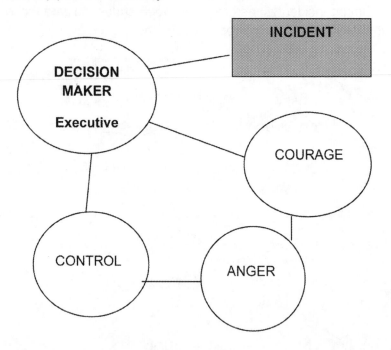

It is quite clear that ANGER is still there; however, with DECISION MAKER in executive, David will draw on the states of COURAGE and CONTROL to move through the incident. Unexpressed anger becomes toxic, unhealthy and there is imbalanced when it is not recognised, experienced or expressed. When this happens, anger becomes underlying, causing internal pressure. When the pressure becomes too great, the emotion comes bubbling up to executive state and one can be seen as out of control, without clarity, direction or intent and without the support of other states. An executive state reshuffle is needed to create a healthy, clear change in behaviour to relate better with others.

David's original states had supported him for a long time, and it wasn't up to me at any point to cast judgements of negativity. David took charge of the 'change process', with me as the navigator. Seeing his State Map written up in front of him was a powerful awakening for this man, as well as the other inmates who were quietly observing, and he had no hesitation in re-creating a more positive State Map for the future. This easy identification for David of the many parts of him gave him a powerful insight into his strengths.

Every state exists within us for a reason and came into being for a reason. It is said that it is incorrect to ask a state to leave; rather it is better to ask it to take on the role of underlying state and be non functioning (think of it as taking a holiday). Or, we could suggest that a state change its roles and, in doing so, it would need to take on a new identity, i.e; being renamed to better suit the new roles. In my experience, when a person chooses to change the roles of a state, they want to change the name of the state to better support the new roles.

For example, one suggestion that David made was that he wanted to change one of the roles in RAGE from 'to be better than the other person' to 'it's okay to hear two opinions'. When we discussed how this then worked with 'being able to be heard' and 'allowing him to let off steam' he decided that the state of RAGE needed a new name, and he changed it to

WIN/WIN. This meant that when WIN/WIN was in executive, his behaviour would be quite different to when the old state of RAGE had been in executive.

Recognising anger is the first step toward effective anger management. A critical part of the process of managing anger is our ability to name our anger and take ownership of it. Anger is just one state to be acknowledged and, as was demonstrated with David's ESI mapping, such states as RAGE and FEAR supported each other and caused inappropriate behaviour.

I can say for certain that my work with prison inmates using ESI and their responses to it have been outstandingly positive. For some it has been an acknowledgment of themselves, of how they have behaved in the past and a look at how they want to behave in future. Obviously, there is the question of 'will they'? This, of course, still has to be put to the test when they are again 'on the outside'; however, there are many opportunities to practise while remaining in prison. To me, positive reinforcement is that they want to come back to my sessions to learn more about themselves and to feel that they can create a chance for change to occur. For me, this work is most gratifying and I will share more stories throughout this book. My work in prisons will continue; in fact, I view it as a never ending story.

Instigating Behavioural Change

Where anger is part of our workplace behavioural repertoire, we are witness to executives and staff acting out in the same way as my inmates, without the same incarcerated outcomes. We know that organisations suffer damage as a consequence of the inappropriate behaviour of staff, whether it is anger or another negative emotional state that is in executive.

Behaviour based on anger is highly motivated and mostly supported by other negative states. Similarly, behaviours motivated by positive states are supported by other positive states. Just as Mary in my earlier story was motivated to behave in a positive way to achieve her goal, a staff member could be motivated by similar positive states to achieve a goal of positively serving a customer.

Whatever the life situation, we are constantly behaving according to the motivation of our executive states. And, because we have many states from which we can choose at any given time, it is possible to learn to change from a state that feels angry and out of control to a state that has a feeling of wellbeing or calmness.

Learning to make positive choices and deciding from which executive state to operate is about being aware of ourselves in any given moment. It is about being aware of the many parts of you and operating from the part that, at times, is focussed on working; at times is playful and laughing; at times is in pain and at times is illogical in feeling and reaction.

There are occasions when you may feel like a different person in attitude, logic and emotion. In fact, you are a single person who is experiencing a number of different states, each with its own personal roles of power, weakness, logic and other personal traits.

When we catch ourselves saying, "Part of me wants to . . .", we are talking about a state inside of us. For 22 years, Mary in my previous story (Chapter One) had a constant battle with her states, when part of her wanted to meet with her daughter and part of her didn't. The state that was the 'didn't want to meet her daughter' was in executive until the motivation surged her into an executive state reshuffle, allowing an underlying state to take on an executive role. She then truly focussed on wanting to meet her daughter.

Similarly, prison inmates, corporate executives, staff members and maybe even you, yourself, behave inappropriately at times! From what state are you choosing to behave in that given moment? Is the state supporting the pathway to your goals or is it holding you back?

Seeing a map of your states written on a sheet of paper in front of you allows you to clearly define the states that make you unique, and also allows acknowledgment and clarity that will enhance behavioural changes and ensure success for you.

My suggestion is to develop your own State Map when disharmony is occurring and then give yourself the right 'self-talk' to create the positive outcomes you desire in your life. Communicate from your executive states and become focussed on achieving success. Ask for the state that wants you to be an achiever to come into executive and remain there until the goal is achieved. Be aware of the reasons the states are there (their roles) and note them down in a journal or note book. Ask the states that don't want you to achieve success to identify their roles and write these onto the same page. I guarantee that this exercise will help you to find the answers (and maybe even the questions) you are looking for—I suggest you give it a try.

Be aware of the "me" that you are on the inside and make positive behavioural changes, where necessary, to support the other "me" that everyone sees.

Chapter Four—ESI in the Workplace

When ESI is used effectively in the workplace it will:

o   Increase staff morale
o   Decrease internal conflict
o   Increase revenue
o   Decrease staff turnover
o   Increase productivity
o   Decrease staff absenteeism
o   Plus much more . . .

When ESI is used in conjunction with training, coaching, facilitation or one-on-one consultations, it can bring about behavioural change that supports new ideas, projects or simply individual self-development.

My work has provided me with multiple opportunities to interact with a variety of people in many different situations. Working with senior management, frontline staff, administrative staff in businesses, school students and inmates in prisons, the one thing I've discovered is that there are a host of similarities which intertwine us. In other words, there are many times when our executive states and our 'State Maps' are similar, sometimes the same. The major difference is the roles of the states in each individual and this is part that gives us our uniqueness.

What senior manager would ever compare themselves to a criminal? What young school student would assume that their values, beliefs, dreams and desire resembled, in any way, that of a corporate giant? My work has revealed many valuable experiences and throughout this book I will share some of them with you.

Workplace harmony is workplace bliss!

When it exists, the workplace is a great place to be. Staff morale is high and, in general, productivity is increased—which in turn leads to an increase in revenue and a decrease in staff turnover. Keeping well-trained, positive staff members adds to the overall success of any business; there is less workplace conflict and more harmonious attempts are made to work together to achieve success. New staff settle in quicker and become 'infected' with the high morale within the company. Workplace bliss continues!

Now for the reality check. How many workplaces are like the description above? If yours is, congratulations! Don't leave! Many workplaces are held back from achieving ultimate success due to workplace 'bitching' and conflict. We are each unique individuals who come together in a workplace because we share certain skills and knowledge, or because we complement each other's skills and knowledge. Our uniqueness allows us to be who we are and also attracts (or detracts) relationships into our lives.

Workplace relationships, in themselves, are unique. I have often said that "we don't have to take our work colleagues home with us and live with them, we just have to work with them"! Workplace harmony is about having good relationships in a business environment that doesn't necessarily equate to socialising. While a certain amount of 'socialising' is considered to be acceptable, and is, in fact, good for staff morale, most bosses like to see staff working rather than chatting in the tea room, or around the water cooler. I'm sure you would agree?

There is no magic wand to wave over the workplace to totally eliminate conflict. However, there are many different strategies one can use, ranging from one-on-one workplace counselling to coaching or effective group training sessions that deal with conflict resolution and effective communication skills. If staff members are open and ready to accept suggestions from training, coaching or counselling and prepared to put these skills into practice, then successful workplace harmony can be achieved.

Alternatively, an ESI process identifies the reason for the disharmony in an individual and promotes the opportunity for that person to work toward resolving conflicts. Using the ESI process, it is a good idea to establish a goal first. This will provide a focus, and then the process of exploring the states of that staff member, together with the roles of those states, begins.

Warning: If you are unqualified in the ESI process it could be dangerous to proceed down the path of developing a State Map. You never know what state may reveal itself and it could be difficult for an inexperienced person to handle. A suggestion is to simply talk to the person about their many parts. Ask them what part of them supports this conflict, for example, and develop a conversation rather than a State Map. Think of ESI as a 'way of talking' to another person, asking about the part of them that supports this behaviour. When we talk about 'the part of us' it is like moving outside of ourselves to identify our part (state). Some have described it as speaking in the third person. Speaking from the position of third person is less threatening and less derogatory for the person.

It is probably best explained by an example.

Tracey worked for a large organisation that had many departments. She had been there for three years. She described feeling depressed about going to work and, rather than enjoying her time there, was becoming a '9-5-er'—arriving and leaving strictly according to her hours. She described that she was experiencing workplace conflict with a group of three women in her section, one in particular. These three women were called, as she described, the workplace 'bitches' and, according to Tracey, would seek out their prey by finding the most vulnerable and seemingly pick on them for little reason. They had each been with the organisation for some time and appeared to 'get away with more' than any of the other staff members did. They were confrontational and outspoken, even to their supervisor.

Tracey was a dedicated worker who rarely took days off and adhered to workplace schedules. On one occasion, Tracey was late back from lunch (which had been pre-approved by her supervisor) and one of the women found an opportunity to make sarcastic remarks in front of others—to Tracey's sheer embarrassment. Despite knowing that she hadn't done anything wrong, Tracey's reaction (embarrassment) seemed to add fuel to the sarcasm.

Tracey's internalisation of this incident, coupled with other ongoing comments, was making her more and more anxious and depressed. Depression is often the result of one or more states feeling isolated, misunderstood, and hopeless. These states need to be able to express their needs directly and to feel heard, understood and respected. These states hold onto energy, refusing to use it or allow it to be used by other states. Holding on to this energy, along with negative feelings, prevents the person from being able to properly engage with others.

Tracey had spoken with her supervisor, who was aware of the disharmony in the workplace, and who also agreed to speak with the other woman—little was achieved! Of course, the other woman denied making any comments and said that Tracey was overreacting. This, of course, did nothing to resolve the workplace issue; in fact, it made it worse. Tracey realised that she needed to take a look at her own processing mechanisms for overcoming this workplace situation and rise above it.

It was a delightful experience to work with Tracey on her goal to become victorious at work, as opposed to being the victim. As she focussed on her goal she began to acknowledge her states and gave most of them the names of colours for recognition. Below is her goal and some of her states:

Goal: To allow the snide remarks of others to bounce off me

CHARCOAL
Role:

- o Unhinge any beliefs of success
- o Put things off
- o Reflection in a mirror

YELLOW
Role:

- o Okay to receive offensive comments
- o Okay to be subservient
- o Okay to be inactive
- o Unhelpful

BLOOD RED
Role:

- o Miserable
- o I'm no good
- o Dark
- o Not fun to be around

DOUBT
Role:

- o Doubt everything
- o Questioning
- o Doubt belongs at work

And then on the *positive* side we found . . .

DEEP PURPLE
Role:

- o To be confident
- o To believe in myself
- o To feel sure of myself
- o To feel good
- o To speak out if I want to
- o To feel balanced and well-rounded

MULTI COLOURED
Role:

- o To feel carefree
- o To have good feelings all the time
- o To be happy and feel freedom

MOTIVATION
Role:

- o Adrenalin boost
- o Remind me of how good it feels to have power
- o Have a sense of accomplishment
- o Energised

Tracey was allowing CHARCOAL, YELLOW, BLOOD RED and DOUBT into executive regularly when at work and was holding on to the energy of these states, giving them power. The other states such as DEEP PURPLE, MULTI COLOURED and MOTIVATION also had power and supported her on other occasions. We discussed a time when she knew that her positive states were in executive and working in her favour and she described times when she played squash and touch football in the winter months. When asked what it would take to allow the positive states to move into executive at work, Tracey agreed that it was a mind-shift into believing that she was doing this for herself, not for anyone else.

What a powerful statement—'doing it for myself"—one that enabled Tracey to make the necessary shift back into achieving workplace harmony for herself. She understood that those other women were on their own journey pathways, which weren't the same as hers, and nothing they could do or say could overturn her focus on her workplace goal—which was to become victorious.

Having an awareness of our states allows the 'self-talk' process to be more powerful and meaningful for us. Interestingly, when I met with Tracey one week after our initial discussion, and then again three weeks after that, we found that other parts of her life had changed, too. She had set one part of her life right and other parts had gained momentum.

Tracey had certainly achieved her goal of allowing the snide remarks of others to bounce off her. In doing so she had achieved so much more.

I wasn't invited into her workplace to address any necessary changes, and maybe the women Tracey referred to wouldn't have been willing participants. Sometimes it just isn't possible to change everything; with Tracey we changed what mattered most to her and her success was achieved.

When a scenario such as Tracey's is spelt out one might be tempted to suggest that you could achieve this without an ESI process. I would have to agree; however, for Tracey this workplace situation was consuming her entire life and until she removed herself from it and looked within—with the help of ESI—there appeared for her to be no way out!

ESI in a training environment

In 2006, I conducted a series of training sessions, run over a five week period for a group of people who had come from a variety of differing workplaces, all working to achieve Certificate IV in Training and Assessment. The group were already bonded when I joined them as the trainer; they had completed one section of the course and my place was to teach the design and delivery components. They were a delightful group of people with many different skills and abilities to share with each other.

There was one particular guy, Paul, who was outspoken at what I considered inappropriate times and causing unnecessary disruption. I spoke with Paul privately over a coffee about his behaviour and saw no change. I tolerated his behaviour with the group up until the third day, when it was quite clear that it was causing other members to become disgruntled and irritated. During a short presentation given by another team member to the group, Paul's outspokenness was just too much. I was sitting as part of the group at one of the tables and the group was becoming uncomfortable for themselves and the person giving the presentation. I addressed him openly across the room, asking him about the part of him that liked to speak out. He was aware of this part and defended it well. I then asked him about the part of him that was sensible and a cooperative team player. This part he also knew and he spoke with a different tone of voice when he acknowledged that state. I asked; *'what would it take to leave that sensible, cooperative team player state in executive for the remainder of the course?',* and with a shrug of the shoulders he agreed to do so, and did!

Neither Paul, nor the rest of the group, knew anything about ESI and I realised I was taking a huge risk in questioning him openly about his states. Whether out of simple embarrassment, or acknowledgement of his states, my goal was accomplished. At the beginning of the following session he approached me and thanked me for bringing to his awareness what he had been doing, he apologised and continued with the course to deliver one of the best presentations for his final assessment, to achieve his Certificate.

Disharmony in teams working towards a particular goal will ultimately cause the process to be hampered or, worse still, prevent the goal from being achieved. The process of ESI can be used with dysfunctional teams to identify the reasons for the dysfunction and seek cooperation to make the necessary adjustments to achieve the goal. It takes a willing team (one that is ready to participate openly in the ESI process), and an experienced ESI Practitioner who can identify the many parts of the team, and the overall results can be outstanding.

The key to success, when working with teams, is to have an ESI Practitioner facilitating the process, to ensure that everyone feels acknowledged and heard. To use ESI with teams brings about a sense of transparency and shifts unwillingness into willingness in order to achieve the goal. The results are dynamic and powerful, not only for the team but for the organisation.

ESI in conjunction with behaviour profiles, training & coaching

ESI is a process that supports other processes, such as behavioural profiles, workplace training, coaching and facilitation or one-on-one consultations. ESI can bring about behavioural changes to support new ideas, projects or self-development.

The use of behavioural profiles gives the team member an overview of their preferred working and learning styles and can be a basis for revealing better ways to communicate with each other. This can generate acceptance by the team members of themselves and others and forms a base line from which to work and to make changes. Behavioural profiling is a great way to identify the best person for the task and to acknowledge and accept the strengths of others. Once a team has a focussed goal they can nominate appropriate team members for a variety of tasks with the confidence that they are operating from the correct executive state to achieve the team goal. Understanding or having awareness or your own style isn't an assured guarantee of bringing about change. When you incorporate an ESI process with a behaviour profile, what needs to change in the individual becomes more obvious and, in most cases, behaviour change occurs.

So, when would it be necessary to ESI a team?

If the team was seen to be moving off task or if team disruption occurred; perhaps some unresolved conflict or an unwillingness to participate by one or more of the team members was the cause. Difficulties within the team can be caused by differences in ideas or philosophy, problems in communication and individual problems that may impinge on the team's effectiveness. I am sure you can think of a time when a team was off task, lost its focus or experienced disruptions. Sometimes these are just 'road humps' to achieving success. However, other times they are monumental and hinder progress. ESI is there to enhance self-awareness and awareness of others, and to promote goal achievement. ESI is not an intervention that is aimed toward changing ideas or philosophy; it is useful to look at differences in ideas that can cause problems in a team. Good communication is imperative for good team development.

Effective communication between team members when using the ESI process means that executive states must be able to speak with a state of another team member and hear and understand what needs to be said.

An angry state of one team member may not effectively speak to a defensive state of another team member. The result of this could be that the angry state would have the sense of being unheard and resented and could consequently feel angrier, while the defensive state of the other team member could simply feel attacked. If a team member has a need to speak from an angry state to another team member, the other team member would need to listen from an understanding state without getting upset. The understanding state does not have to agree with what the angry state is saying, but it does need to have the intelligence to show an understanding of the other person's point of view.

Anger, in itself, is an interesting state. Anger is an emotion, not behaviour, yet is often described as the way in which a person behaves. There are two distinct problems concerning anger; a person can have a problem *not releasing anger* or a problem with the *way* in which they release anger. Not releasing anger can create internal psychological distress, and the inappropriate release of anger can create external sociological problems, particularly in the workplace. The inappropriate release of anger can result in psychological anxiety.

Holding on to anger can result in passive-aggressive behaviour, physical distress or even panic attacks. When I speak with a person who presents to me in this way, state identification can enable negotiation for changing the roles of those states that have learned to hang on to the anger over a number of years. An angry state can learn to communicate better with an assertive state so the anger can be released in a more appropriate way. Every identified state in this process needs to be satisfied with any arrangement of roles.

When anger is inappropriately expressed, particularly in the workplace, it is important that we talk to the state that needs to change. It is little use talking only to the state that gets angry because it may feel that it had a right to become angry when things didn't go as planned. Talking to the other states involved in supporting the executive role of the angry state is equally important to optimise the opportunity for appropriate behavioural change to occur.

State negotiation would be considered the right approach once all the states are identified. Once again, an agreement from all states would be necessary.

ESI TEAMS ARE HIGH PERFORMANCE TEAMS

A team is more than just a group of individuals who work together. A team is a small number of individuals with complementary skills committed to a common purpose, common performance goals, and an approach for which they hold themselves collectively accountable.

Tasks or situations that lend themselves to the use of a team require a combination of knowledge, expertise, and perspective that cannot be found in a single individual. To be part of a team requires individuals to be highly interdependent to get their work done to achieve their common goal. They function best by building a strong performance ethic which is critical to encouraging team performance.

The successful performance of a team depends on the collective performances of individual members of the team. Much of this flows from the synergy of the team members' assembled skills and experiences. In addition, teams tend to establish new communication processes that allow for ongoing problem-solving. Many people enjoy, and are motivated by, working in teams. As a result, they deliver their best performance in a team.

Skills and knowledge alone will not allow a team to deliver its very best, other factors, such as individual attitudes, beliefs and values, have a huge impact upon the high performance (or under performance) of a team. The question then arises: how do we know that each team member shares attitudes of a positive nature, with beliefs that are focussed on the end goal and values that align with other team members, together with the values of the company?

A fully functional team is one where 'all parts of individual members are aligned to the common goal', therefore, 'all parts of the team are aligned to the achievement of the common goal'.

Individually, we often struggle to deliver our best, particularly when a part of us is not truly focussed. Individual attitudes and beliefs impact upon the team focus and drive, which in turn reflects on the performance of the entire team. When such things as trust, respect and competence (for example) are challenged, individuals will not perform to their very best and enthusiasm will wain, relationships will fail and productivity will be grossly affected.

So, how do you maintain high levels of motivation when 'parts of the team' are struggling?

ESI® the team!

ESI® is a strategic Mapping Tool that defines the factors of the team and classifies them into three areas—Supportive, Inhibiting and Irrelevant. Using a specially designed **ES® Card Sort**, team members are able to qualify factors that can be attributed to the success and/or failure of a team's performance.

All too often our thoughts are steered toward all positive aspects of success. While this is well and good, if there is a 'part of an individual' who is screaming beneath the surface because they don't feel empowered or appreciated for their efforts, the impact upon the overall success of the team could bring about disastrous results.

How does this work?

A team is gathered together, with the common goal quite clearly identified. Individuals are given a set of **ES® Cards** and asked to sort through the specially chosen words and clearly identify what each word on the card means to them in relation to the common goal and the team. After this process the Factor Intensity Scale is used and then the team collectively evaluates the words and their impact on achieving the goal.

From here, the pathway is clear to proceed in a more positive way towards goal achievement.

Conclusion

If your team is failing to meet the benchmarks set in place, or if you suspect disharmony in your team, you can be assured that the team is not performing to peak performance. A team that has been "**ESI**®'d" will be a productive, high-performing team, one that enjoys healthy relationships and success in abundance.

Chapter Five—Case Studies

This chapter is dedicated to discussing more case studies of the wonderful clients who have approached me over the years, wanting to make changes to their lives. Some clients have been seeking counselling while others have engaged my services as a coach or have been seeking greater workplace harmony. In every instance recited here, the ESI process has been used to identify executive states, acknowledge their roles and develop a map of the person's states. There have been some occasions where it has been necessary to induce a light state of hypnosis to relax the client further and elicit stubborn underlying states to be identified, in order to assist the client make their desired changes. Their stories are, without exception, inspirational.

Jan Sky

Julie

Support Teacher

I met Julie in 2006, when she was in her late thirties. Julie had a teenage son and was about to marry for the second time. She worked at a school supporting students with learning disabilities and had been working casually in this role for 14 years. There was an opportunity for her to become a permanent staff member of the school and that meant applying for the job through regular channels and going through the interview process. Her CV was superb and gave a clear indication of her abilities and experience working in this area. However, it was the interview process that scared her as she felt that her fear would override any other parts of her that desired to appear confident and capable in front of the interview panel.

Goal: I am confident and capable and will gain a permanent position at the school

During our discussion she revealed two executive states that she loved to operate from:

CONFIDENCE
Role:

- o Shine in groups
- o Feel good about myself
- o Enjoy life
- o Do what I need to do

OUTGOING
Role:

- o Approach people
- o Bridge conversation gaps

o   Interact in groups
o   Interact with peers

When Julie was in these executive states she really shone and when she spoke about them her body language changed, reflecting a more confident position in the chair and she spoke with confidence. If she was to get through this interview and be successful, she needed to bring them both into executive at appropriate times. Both of the states supported each other and knew about each other's existence.

There was, however, another state that held her back and that was the state of:

FEAR
Role:

o   Made her feel sick
o   Felt stress
o   Made her feel unhappy

The state of FEAR wasn't liked by the other two executive states and certainly when FEAR was in executive CONFIDENCE and OUTGOING became non executive. FEAR had been with Julie on previous occasions. She described to me a time she remembered when she was a child of about two years of age. Her parents had been fighting and she didn't know what to do. She was scared of the dynamics in the house and felt unsupported and unloved. Thinking from the mind of a two year old, FEAR was an appropriate executive state given the circumstances of the time and yet, with further discussion, we established that the state of FEAR didn't belong in the interview room in the forthcoming situation. Today as a woman in her 30s the FEAR state of a two year old was inappropriate.

I asked her what it would take for FEAR to become an underlying state that was non functioning over the next few days and, in particular, during the interview. She replied that if CONFIDENCE and OUTGOING could work together in executive, FEAR could do that. We created a 'self-talk' dialogue that she could repeat to herself whenever she felt the signs of FEAR creeping into her functioning state.

Julie's self-talk dialogue was:

"I am a confident, outgoing person who interacts well during interview"

Julie went for the interview and, using CONFIDENCE and OUTGOING, was successful in gaining the permanent position.

By acknowledging what was going on for her, identifying her states and their roles, and then creating a self-talk dialogue unique to Julie, she was able to process and push through inhibiting barriers to achieve success.

Note: There may have been times in your life where you faced an interview situation similar to Julie's. Maybe you had the skills and confidence to push through and win. Or maybe, like Julie, with a little help to identify a State Map and acknowledge those inappropriate states holding you back, you could have easily identified the appropriate states that would ensure your success. Julie's FEAR state came from a situation that occurred over 30 years ago, and yet she was still using it today.

When were your states that are inappropriate and don't support you in life today born?

Carla

Staying focussed and in the present moment

I met Carla in October 2006 and she was struggling with staying focussed in the present moment. Her area of work was in money exchange and, although she believed in her ability to build her business beyond its current level of success, she spent a lot of time reflecting on her past. Carla described her past as being neither successful nor praising of her talents; it was a past where she struggled to be recognised as being 'good enough' at anything she did. Today she was looking forward and, in recognising her talents in the money exchange area, knew that she needed to stay focussed in the present moment. She was tired of being caught up in the habit of reflecting on the past—a past that hadn't served her well.

Carla's situation is interesting because she not only identified several states and their associated roles, she gave a name change to one state, and eliminated some of the roles.

I've set Carla's State Map out below:

Goal: I stay focussed and am in the present

LONELINESS
Roles:

- o Remember how much she hurts
- o Don't rely on other people

SUCCESS
Roles:

- o Hasn't achieved enough
- o Can be detrimental

o   Confuses her about what success really is
o   Look at others

PEACEFUL
Roles:

o   Content with who Carla is
o   Slow down to achieve
o   See beauty and abundance

ALONE
Roles:

o   Needs to look at herself
o   She hasn't found anyone to give her guidance
o   There's no role model
o   Can run her own race
o   Has motivation

ALONE was the state that changed its name to INNER STRENGTH and some of the roles were eliminated.

INNER STRENGTH (once ALONE)

Roles:

o   Needs to look at herself
o   Look within for guidance
o   Needs no role model
o   Can run her own race
o   Has motivation

During discussions with Carla, we established that LONELINESS belonged in her past and that SUCCESS was part of her future. PEACEFUL and the newly named role of INNER STRENGTH worked together in order for her to achieve success.

Her self-talk dialogue was created:

"My inner strength keeps me focussed, I am a success"

For Carla, seeing a map of her states written on a sheet of paper in front of her allowed her to clearly define the states that made up who she was. She expressed to me that this gave her acknowledgement and clarity that enhanced behavioural changes and she felt confident about moving forward and remaining successful.

We met on two more occasions after this first visit to ensure she was on track with her work and also that she was using the correct states to achieve this.

I saw Carla six months after our initial visits and she was pleased to report her successes and was continuing to move forward spending very little time these days dwelling in the past.

Daniel

Weight loss

I was introduced to Daniel in 2001, and we met occasionally at business meetings. Daniel is a successful businessman with a company that was taking business overseas; his business was becoming recognised as an industry leader. He originally approached me because he wanted to reduce his weight and, as our conversation progressed, we established that his overweight frame was inhibiting his progress in many aspects of his life—personally and at work.

His State Map is identified below:

Goal: I sustain overall good health and fitness that promotes my wellbeing

The first state he identified was:

SLOB
Roles:

- o   To watch TV
- o   Sit around
- o   Do nothing

Other states we identified were:

WINNER
Roles:

- o   To achieve at work
- o   To achieve with his health

STRONG
Roles:

o   Strong in body and mind
o   Work hard
o   Achieve good health

THINKER
Roles:

o   To be the driver
o   To drive activities such as, walking, working in the gardens and garage
o   To be analytical of all things

It became obvious to Daniel that WINNER, STRONG and THINKER knew each other and worked together to achieve success. His current business was certainly proof of that; however, when SLOB was in executive and active, the other three were discouraged from being active and became non executive states. Daniel knew how easy it was to be in the executive state of SLOB but he also knew how focussed he was on achieving his primary goal. He had recently turned 50 and was looking forward to a healthy future where he could enjoy life more fully with his wife and two grown daughters.

A dialogue was created to reinforce the activities of WINNER, STRONG and THINKER and with my next meeting with Daniel, I learned that he was making more positive choices about his food and activities and he had already lost two kilos. Daniel continued to achieve outstanding results and is extremely pleased with his success.

Daniel's self-talk dialogue was:

"My strong winning ways promote my healthy, fit wellbeing"

Rita

Customer Service Manager

Rita worked for a large government organisation and was one of the company's senior managers. She approached me expressing anxiety about being overworked and said she had developed an inability to concentrate and stay focussed. Rita was taking a lot of work home with her, which she resented, because home was the place to enjoy the company of her husband and young son. She was also having trouble with her organisational and time management skills and this was an area of frustration, as it impeded her progress.

Rita was a perfectionist and liked to check everything at least twice to ensure her work was perfect before letting it go. This checking and rechecking process attributed to her poor time management. By visiting me she hoped to become more trusting of her own abilities, and therefore delegate to others and pass her work on to management in a quicker time frame.

Goal: I am more organised and less stressed, maintaining balance and harmony between work and home

Rita's states were identified in this way:

MISS CONFIDENT
Roles:

- o   I know what I'm doing
- o   I know my job
- o   I'm the only one who knows
- o   I'm sure of what I can do
- o   Ability to sleep

MISS ORGANISED
Roles:

o I can organise a cat out of the bag
o Keep drawers neat and tidy
o Keep papers in order

MISS WRITER
Roles:

o To work with Miss Confidence and Miss Organised
o To write
o To communicate in writing

MISS RELAXED
Roles:

o Engaged on the weekend
o Engaged at night time
o At work
o There to have lunch
o Go for a walk
o To re-learn piano

MISS CUDDLY
Roles:

o To be cuddled
o Tell husband I love him

All of the above states Rita identified as positive and executive states she loved to be in. They supported her through life and were each aware of one another. An interesting point was revealed when we identified MISS RELAXED, and that was that Rita really wanted to take piano lessons. She didn't own a piano so wasn't sure at this point what she would do with regard to practice, but it was certainly a strong role of this state.

In addition to these positive states, Rita also identified the following states:

MUDDLER
Roles:

- o Confuse her
- o Keep her from being organised
- o Don't let her take control
- o Keep her from organising everybody

UNSURE
Roles:

- o Make it difficult to make a decision
- o Help her procrastinate
- o See good and bad in everything

COMMON SENSE
Roles:

- o Know that's the way to go
- o Logic

With further discussion, we identified that MUDDLER and UNSURE needed to go because Rita knew that she was a person with ability and was capable of high achievements. A recent company nomination as *'staff member most likely to succeed'* confirmed that and she knew that staying in the executive state of MUDDLER and UNSURE gave her no credibility. In fact, she told me that when she was in the states of MUDDLER and UNSURE she questioned why her company bothered to nominate her with the title! She wanted these two states 'kicked out' and we proceeded to develop a self-talk dialogue to enhance the other positive states in executive.

Note: Getting rid of a state completely, in my experience, hasn't worked effectively. States are there for a reason and came into existence at a particular point in a person's life. Asking a state to move into an underlying role has proven much more successful and this is what I did with Rita's states of UNSURE and MUDDLER.

We reinforced the power of MISS CONFIDENT, MISS ORGANISED, MISS WRITER and MISS RELAXED and she told me that what she described as her 'Rita-isms' were linked to COMMON SENSE and it was important for her to put COMMON SENSE into executive more often.

Self-talk dialogue:

> *"Miss Confident, Organised, Writer and Relaxed listen to Common Sense and I have balance and harmony in my life"*

A Christmas card from Rita thanked me for the help I had given her over the past few months and included a special note to say that she had hired a piano, was taking lessons and would be playing a Christmas Carol for me.

Shayley

Young business entrepreneur

Shaley is a successful business owner in the area of manufacturing. She is in her late 30s and had run a chain of businesses overseas for many years, before selling them and returning to Australia with her partner of five years. He also worked in the business with her. Shaley was looking to move her business 'to the next level', she explained. The business' success at the moment was okay, but she identified that there was room for growth and she struggled to define what was holding her back.

Goal: My business has moved to the next level

Identified states were:

LOVE
Roles:

- o Real me
- o What it's all about
- o To change things
- o Help other people
- o Make things better
- o Be peaceful

ANGRY
Roles:

- o To protect me
- o To think bad things
- o Allow me to be negative
- o Stand up for myself

CONFUSED
Roles:

- o Don't know
- o Make things difficult
- o Calm

Together, we wrote down these states and their roles and discussed how they aligned with achieving her goal. Shaley decided to make some changes to the roles and, in doing so, gave them new names. LOVE became the PRESIDENT and the roles stayed the same, however ANGRY became VICE PRESIDENT—ASSERTIVE and the roles of 'to think bad things' and 'allow me to be negative' were eliminated and replaced with 'to help me exercise and be physical'.

Two days after her visit to me, I received an email from Shaley thanking me for the amazing experience and explaining that, by using her self-talk dialogue, business results were visible the next day. A deal with a client that she had been working on for a couple of months all of a sudden became a reality. Her company sent out five orders the day before and had received another three orders that day, with a request to quote for 20-24,000 products. This was an unusually high product order and Shaley was extremely excited.

She described how the new VP (formerly known as ANGRY) acted as a drill sergeant in the morning when she and her partner went for their walk and, instead of her walking the staircase at the beach (while he ran it), she ran it with him. Then the crunch came! The new VP—ASSERTIVE decided it was time to speak up about an issue with her partner that she had been mulling over for some time. However, he (not used to the new Shaley yet) was shocked and she described how he had become very sullen ever since.

Making behavioural changes will affect who you are. It is not possible to stay the same and change behaviour; changing behaviour changes who you are and how you are seen by others.

Consequently, this has an effect on those around you, as it did with Shaley and her partner. It was a shock for her partner to hear her speak out about personal issues so strongly. Fortunately, Shaley and I had the opportunity to discuss this situation at a second meeting and it was possible for me to reinforce her new-found inner strength and courage so she could allow PRESIDENT and VP to be in executive in the workplace, and LOVE could be in executive with her partner out of the workplace.

A further email arrived after our second meeting, informing me that she was feeling wonderful and building up to "even-betterness" (a new word she just invented). She disclosed that she was feeling a tiny bit scared, or maybe more nervous, about the changes that had taken place and the changes that she was still aware were happening, but was prepared to pursue this new awareness.

Her new self-talk dialogue:

> *"The President and VP control my workplace and Love is with me always"*

Shaley is a 'work in progress', as we will meet on many more occasions for coaching to discuss her business ventures and future goals.

Sam

Young business franchise owner

Sam was a career-minded woman with a young family and a husband supportive of her business choices. Sam had just purchased a business franchise and was working frantically to maintain its success.

Her working day was long, starting at 5am and often finishing well into the night if she had an evening appointment. Sam had developed a habit of pouring that glass of wine every night when she walked in the door, nibbling on a few chips or crackers and dip while preparing the evening meal and then consuming a larger than normal portion of food for dinner, along with another glass of wine or two or three, and sometimes a bowl of ice cream before going to bed! Slowly, the kilos were beginning to show and although she was aware of the correct eating regime and a daily exercise program, the evening food intake would undo any good she may have done during the day.

Her goal was to become a healthy evening eater and eliminate the need for regularly drinking wine, reserving this for special functions. By doing this she would eventually lose the extra kilos, but initially we needed to address the immediate goal of a better evening food intake and regular exercise.

Sam's State Map revealed that there was one state that was acting in executive regularly and she called this state SAM. The role of SAM was to rationalise, to lead her to make the right decisions and know what to do.

Another state she called DECISION MAKER was a 9-5 working state. Its role was to weigh up the pros and cons, put forward the evidence and process the right decisions.

A third state was identified as CAREER, and its role was to look after her and keep her healthy, and to ensure she exercised regularly, ate correctly and took her prescribed medication.

All of these states knew of and supported each other and went in and out of executive, depending on the situation.

However, there was another state that was revealed, which she called GUILT. The role of GUILT was to make her feel bad when doing wrong and to give her a sense of uncertainty. GUILT was strong and had come into executive about six years before, when a certain life situation presented itself to her. The situation had caused her to feel a sense of guilt for neglecting her husband and family while pursuing her own interests. When GUILT was in executive it was the state that was responsible for over-eating and drinking each night.

Once we had a visual map of her states, Sam became aware of the need to move DECISION MAKER from 9-5 to a state that operated constantly, and for it to work in conjunction with CAREER and SAM, in order to overcome the night-time bingeing. These three states were strong and Sam enjoyed life when they were in executive. GUILT was ordered to an underlying state by acknowledging that its purpose was no longer needed in the current-day life situation and a self-talk dialogue was created—*"I am focussed on my career and make the right decisions for my life every day in every way"*.

Sam visited me on two more occasions and I saw her a few months after our state mapping had been completed. She was excited to tell me about how well she was doing and how fit she was feeling as a result of the exercise routine she was maintaining. She attributed her success to the time she created her unique map of who she really was.

Bailey

When alcohol affects relationships

Bailey was a client who had a problem with drinking. He held down a responsible job and only drank in the evenings and on social occasions. The problem was that his partner of 15 years drank very rarely and would usually have only one social glass of wine when they dined out. Bailey's frequent drinking meant that the nights were lonely for his partner; retiring early leaving him to fall asleep on the lounge and, some time during the night, crawl into bed. It wasn't every night, just enough nights to make life uncomfortable for him and his partner. Bailey knew his behaviour wasn't acceptable and recognised that it was damaging the relationship.

Goal: I drink only when out and in appropriate company

Identified states were:

SENSIBLE ONE
Roles:

- o Control
- o Think through responses
- o Shape everything
- o Work
- o Walk dogs
- o Cook

JUDGE
Roles:

- o Control
- o Criticise
- o Be analytical
- o Have compassion

ANGER
Roles:

- o Don't care what you think
- o Don't take responsibility
- o Don't tell me what to do
- o Do what I want regardless of consequences

ESCAPIST
Roles:

- o Stop him from thinking
- o Stop him from worrying
- o Feel good
- o Avoid responsibility

SADNESS
Roles:

- o Help him know about hurt
- o Work escapist up

We discovered that JUDGE and SENSIBLE ONE knew each other and worked well for Bailey and, when they were in executive, he was strong and could take control of his thoughts and actions. The three states that held him back from achieving his goals were ESCAPIST, ANGER and SADNESS.

Bailey decided that if there was a name change of ESCAPIST to RELAXED, that state could carry the same roles; however, SADNESS wouldn't be able to support ESCAPIST because, in name, it was gone.

Then he came up with an extensive self-talk dialogue that went like this:

"I choose not to drink at home and to honour the relationship with my partner",

"I acknowledge my weight and drink less for a healthier body and mind",

"I drink only when out in appropriate company",

"I make positive choices around my body"

Bailey wrote these dialogue phrases and placed them in specific places such as: wallet, refrigerator, diary and desk-top calendar, as this was his way of addressing the future in the most positive way.

This has been another success story, as Bailey had, for nine months, maintained a low level of alcohol intake and enjoys a better relationship with his partner. Bailey's repertoire of dialogue was spoken individually at appropriate times and apparently worked well for him.

Note: It is not my preference to develop multiple 'self-talk' dialogue for a client; however, in Bailey's case, it appeared to work.

Tom

Chief Engineer

Tom was Chief Engineer of a 5-star hotel in the northern districts of Sydney. He was so proficient at his job that he was often flown to other 5-star hotels interstate to give advice on project strategies and teach others to develop the skills of their trade. He had been with this company for about five years now and, by and large, loved what he did.

Tom's dilemma was whether or not to accept a career change. The career change came from outside the hotel industry and offered an opportunity for him to head an organisation and to run it as if it was his own business. The money was considerably more than he was earning or could possibly earn from his current job. The location was closer to home and it also gave Tom the opportunity to extend himself to his full potential and develop more business acumen and recognition.

Aged 47, Tom was married, with no children. His wife was successfully pursuing her own career in her own business so, for Tom, this was a fantastic opportunity—and yet there was a part of him that couldn't say yes! His states were in conflict and for him to make the right decision, Tom requested to take part in an ESI process with me.

Through a series of simple questions I was able to tease out of Tom what the part of him was that truly wanted this change. He identified this as the part of him that loved a challenge, and agreed that we should just call this state LOVED A CHALLENGE. This executive state had been with Tom since he was a teenager, when he rode fast motor bikes and played at life dangerously. He rather liked this state and his body language was appropriate with shoulders back, chin up, a smile on his face, and a changed tone of voice.

LOVED A CHALLENGE
Roles:

o   Make decisions at work
o   Courage
o   Support him to make decisions around his home life

Tom also identified two other states that communicated well with LOVED A CHALLENGE, and they were STRENGTH and CONFIDENCE. Together, when these three states were in executive, Tom could achieve success. I acknowledged and praised the roles of these states and supported his feelings of achievement.

STRENGTH
Roles:

o   Focussed
o   Determined
o   Positive and negative

CONFIDENCE
Roles:

o   Knew what was right
o   Made him feel strong
o   Outstanding
o   All-knowing

I asked Tom to tell me about the part of him that didn't want this change to occur.

Tom identified a state that had the role of fear. He gave the state the name of FEAR and said that FEAR had been around for some time as well.

FEAR
Roles:

o   To protect me
o   Keep me from falling flat on my face
o   Keep me from being embarrassed in situations

He believed that the part he identified as FEAR was also about the fear of failure. When FEAR was in executive state, Tom just sat back and did nothing much at all. We talked more about FEAR and how it had protected him over the years. FEAR had held him back on many occasions from achieving his goals; and held him back from achieving more success. FEAR was in executive when it was necessary to make important job decisions that contributed to his personal success, yet not there when he made important job decisions in his current job role.

When I asked if there was another state that supported FEAR, he replied that FEAR was strong alone.

So we have identified four states; three that, together, allowed Tom to achieve success and one that protected, or inhibited, success. The question now was about what states were appropriate to enable Tom to make the right decision.

Tom made the decision to stay in his current role as Chief Engineer because when he processed our conversation he realised another two states that hadn't been identified. They were states that had the roles of 'security' and 'supportive to his wife'. These two states worked together and were important for Tom, as he wanted and needed to support his wife so she could take the risks she needed in her growing business and climb the ladder of success. Tom had a desire to join his wife in business in the future and this was something they had already discussed. He acknowledged his state of FEAR and stated that it wasn't a part of the decision making process this time, and he was happy for FEAR to become non functional (move into an underlying role) for the moment.

He was proud of his executive states—LOVED A CHALLENGE, STRENGTH and CONFIDENCE—and this new awareness gave him courage to use these states daily in his current role. Tom was happy knowing that one day his long-term goal would be achieved in the working partnership of his choice.

Using the ESI process Tom alleviated the inner conflict and processed the right outcome for him.

Stepping Beyond the Resistance

From Silvia de Ridder, Unconscious Potential

Mary, herself, was a leadership coach and came with the goal of wanting to commence an exercise program, but lacked motivation to commence and knew something was holding her back. She would think about it, plan it and yet something would get in the way of making it happen. At other times, she would step out of her front door, yet a nagging pain would surface, preventing her from proceeding. Mary described what was going on for her like a "speed hump" and needed to understand what she was resisting.

Using the process of ESI over a series of sessions, we were able to map Mary's supportive and unsupportive factors in respect of her goal. In identifying these factors, we worked to bridge the identified unsupportive factors, shifting their function to an underlying state. The outcome being that Mary *did* commence her exercise program in line with her goal and continued this ongoing activity, as confirmed by a follow-up check in some eight weeks post-session.

Below is Mary's testimonial in relation to the process:

> *"Working with Silvia and the ESI—Executive State Process—gave me the foot hold I needed to climb over one of the last remaining bastions of resistance I had to living my life in flow. Even though I have tried many different processes to find true ease in my goal attainment—I was still experiencing struggle in a few of my goals. A few run throughs of an ESI—Executive State Process with Silvia has me feeling a sense of inner freedom, and with an inspired call to action that I had not experienced previously. I feel energised and*

inspired and the best part is I am getting things done without struggle, just ease."

Mary, Personal Leadership Coach

The ESI Mapping Tool is uniquely powerful in breaking the mold of old patterns and is able to go beneath the surface of entrenched behaviour.

Summary

There are many other ways one can approach this type of decision making process; a simple SWOT analysis or a Pros and Cons sheet for example. However, my belief is, and certainly my many hundreds of case studies prove, that in identifying the parts of you—your unique parts—and teasing out what their roles are, you give personal strength to this type of decision making process. Executive State Identification allows the power of individuality and personal analysis of what is right for you. It also clearly defines states that may have been supportive when used in a past situation, time or place, but inappropriate for the current situation, time or place.

ESI works because it's prescriptive to the individual. A self-talk dialogue created by the individual after they have identified their states provides a powerful reminder of their own unique State Map. States that form the unique part of their being and states that are true for each individual.

Self-talk dialogue has been around for many years and is often more commonly referred to as 'Affirmations'. Self-talk used in a positive sense promotes a healthier mind. Coaches of sporting elites promote the use of self-talk for their pupils and clients to achieve success. You could never imagine an athlete such as Ian Thorpe or Tiger Woods thinking or speaking anything but positive self-talk—it is part of what makes them a success.

When a client uses an ESI process to create a dialogue that is so unique to the individual, by the individual, the self-talk dialogue has much more power.

When clients create their own dialogue it is often necessary to give assistance by turning past tense into present and eliminating negatives. Clients are always happy with a little assistance and agree that, with help, the dialogue becomes more streamlined and easier to remember and say.

Other suggestions are:

- write the 'self-talk' dialogue on a piece of paper and carry it with you, to be viewed regularly
- place the 'self-talk' dialogue in a prominent position so it can be viewed daily
- put it on the fridge, on your desk, in your diary
- tell a trusted friend or partner so they can help you reinforce your behavioural change

Be proactive with your own behaviour change to support an even better you.

ESI

Caring for what is within,

co-existing with what is beyond.

About the author and Business Consultancy Services

After more than 25 years as a corporate trainer, counsellor and Clinical Hypnotherapist, Jan recognised trends that were holding people back from achieving their full potential. From her extensive studies Jan developed **ESI®**, a process that motivates change.

As a perpetual learner, Jan is currently enrolled in a Masters Degree at Sydney University in Health Sciences, specialising in Sexual Health. She understands that ESI® will be of great benefit when practicing in this field, as it currently is in counselling and hypnotherapy.

Jan is proud of her client base, which ranges from prison inmates to senior corporate executives. She is passionate about the study of people and their behaviour and is constantly looking for ways to assist others to make the changes they want in their lives and feel the success which comes with achievement.

Jan's training business was established in 1993 and continues today to operate out of Sydney, Australia, servicing a national and international market. *Sky training* delivers corporate training in the areas of leadership and team development, with a strong focus on developing high-performing people by motivating changes in behaviour. Her executive coaching has been recognised for its outstanding results.

With the evolution of ESI® came business success with more and more organisations wanting to introduce the Mapping Tool to assist with performance appraisals, team building, coaching and performance counselling.

To deliver and work with the ESI Mapping Tool you must be an accredited ESI Partner. To become an ESI Partner it is necessary to complete training and continue to work with the Mapping Tool, gathering case studies.

ESI® TEAMS has evolved to accommodate the needs of groups who want to perform to their full potential.

ESI®TEAMS is a strategic Mapping Tool that defines the factors of the team and classifies them into three areas—Supportive, Inhibiting and Irrelevant. Using a specially designed **ESI® Card Sort**, team members are able to qualify factors that attribute to the success and/or failure of a team's performance.

All too often our thoughts are steered toward all positive aspects of success. While this is well and good, if there is a 'part of an individual' who is screaming beneath the surface because they don't feel empowered or appreciated for their efforts, the impact upon the overall success of the team could bring about disastrous results.

If your team is failing to meet the benchmarks set in place, or if you suspect disharmony in your team, you can be assured that the team is not performing to peak performance. A team that has been "**ESI®**'d" will be a productive, high-performing team, one that enjoys healthy relationships and success in abundance.

For more information, go to:

ESI website: www.execstateid.com.au

or

email jan@skytraining.com.au

or call **1300 787 694** (within Australia)

+61 2 9522 2050 (outside Australia)

+61 2 0409 869 664 (mobile)

NOTES

NOTES

NOTES